SPOTTER'S GUIDE
WILD B

Peter Holden

National Organizer of the Junior Section of the
Royal Society for the Protection of Birds

Illustrated by
Trevor Boyer

Designed by Susannah Owen and Cristina Adami
Edited by Felicity Brooks, Sue Jacquemier and Sue Tarsky
Series Editor: Philippa Wingate
Series Designer: Laura Fearn
Photographs © Digital Vision
Additional illustrations by Chris Shields
Cover illustration © Gardman

This edition published in 2005 by Usborne Publishing
Limited, Usborne House, 83-85 Saffron Hill, London
EC1N 8RT, England. www.usborne.com

Printed in India

Golden
eagle

CONTENTS

HOW TO USE THIS BOOK

This book will help you to identify many of the birds of Britain, Ireland and other parts of Europe. The pictures show birds perching, swimming or flying, depending on how that kind of bird is most often seen.

As well as a colour picture, each bird also has a description to help you to identify it. The pictures are not drawn to scale, but the description gives you the average length of the bird from its beak to its tail.

Kingfisher 17cm

The measurements in this book show how long a bird would be if it were stretched out like this

Buzzards are most often seen in flight

Partridges are most often seen on the ground

Shovelers are usually seen swimming

The description also tells you where to look for the bird. Beside each picture is a small, blank circle. Each time you spot that bird, make a tick in the circle. The example below shows how the birds are drawn and described in this book.

← HOOPOE
Rare visitor to Britain, seen mainly in spring. More common in southern Europe. Probes ground for insects with its long bill. 28cm.

Circle for ticking

WHAT LIVES WHERE
The green area on this map shows the countries covered by this book. Not every bird from each country is in the book, and some are not found everywhere in the green area. The descriptions refer to the British Isles and Ireland, unless another area is named.

Scandinavia

British Isles

Europe

5

WHERE TO WATCH BIRDS

Birds are everywhere, which makes watching them a good hobby. You can start by watching them from a window in your home, or in a garden. If there are only a few birds, try putting out food and water to attract more (see pages 55-56).

When you can identify all the birds near your home, try looking in a local park. School playing fields, old gravel pits and even rubbish tips also attract birds. Always take an adult with you when you go out and make sure you birdwatch safely.

Lakes, ponds and streams are home to ducks, swans, rails and wading birds such as herons. Dippers and wagtails visit fast-flowing streams.

Seashores, cliffs and estuaries attract many species, especially at low tide when birds come to feed. Rocky cliffs provide nest sites.

Each different kind of bird is called a species. If you go away from home, you will be able to see new species when you visit new habitats (places where birds live). These photos show habitats where you may see a wide range of species.

Forests provide nest sites, shelter and food for many birds. Conifers are home to fewer birds than deciduous trees (trees which lose their leaves).

WHAT TO TAKE

When you go out to spot birds, wear comfortable clothes and shoes, suitable for outdoors. Take this book and a notepad and pencil so that you can make notes and sketches to record what you see.

As you do more birdwatching, you will probably want to use binoculars. Visit a good shop and try out several pairs. The best sizes are 8x30 or 8x40 (never more than 10x50 or they will be too heavy).

Make sure your binoculars are light enough to carry around with you.

WHAT TO LOOK FOR

When you are trying to identify a bird, ask yourself these questions: What size and shape is it? What colour is it? Does it have any special markings? Where does it live? How does it feed? How does it fly?

Remember that in some cases the males and females of a species look different from each other. In this book these symbols are used show which is which:

♂ = Male

♀ = Female

Be aware that some species have different plumages (feathers) in summer and winter.

Ruff in summer

Ruff in winter

Female Chaffinch ♀

Male Chaffinch ♂

Juvenile Ringed Plover

Adult Ringed Plover

Also remember that the young birds (juveniles) of some species look different from the adults.

THE PARTS OF A BIRD

Although birds vary from species to species, they all have wings, feathers and a beak. To describe birds accurately, it's useful to know the names of some of their other parts too.

Bands of colour on the wings or tail are known as bars

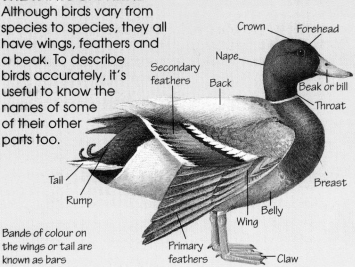

Male mallard

Crown
Forehead
Nape
Secondary feathers
Back
Beak or bill
Throat
Tail
Rump
Breast
Belly
Wing
Primary feathers
Claw

NOTES AND SKETCHES

Try to make sketches of the birds you spot and note down when and where you saw them and what the weather was like. Estimate the length of the bird, or compare it to the size of one you know. Write down its shape and colour, and what it sounds like.

This shows the sort of notes you could make about a male mallard

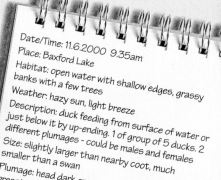

Date/Time: 11.6.2000 9.35am
Place: Baxford Lake
Habitat: open water with shallow edges, grassy banks with a few trees
Weather: hazy sun, light breeze
Description: duck feeding from surface of water or just below it by up-ending. 1 of group of 5 ducks. 2 different plumages - could be males and females
Size: slightly larger than nearby coot, much smaller than a swan
Plumage: head dark green, body two-tone grey, breast chestnut. White ring round neck. Beak yellowy-green. Tail black and white with curly black feathers on top. Legs orange
Shape: typical duck shape
Voice: loud quacks, quiet nasal calls
Conclusion: a male mallard?

SPOTTING RARE BIRDS

Some of the birds in this book may not be very common where you live. Try to spot them if you go away on holiday or on a trip away from home.

Other birds are rare in the wild. You can tick off rare birds if you spot them at a bird reserve or a bird sanctuary, or if you see them on television.

Coasts are good places to see birds, but you should never try to climb cliffs and rocks or cross mud flats. It can be very dangerous.

SHAG, GANNET, CORMORANT

Crest only in nesting season

◀ SHAG
Lives near the sea. Nests in colonies on rocky coasts. Dives for fish. Young are brown. 78cm.

Shags fly low, close to water

⬇ GANNET
Look for gannets out to sea, close to waves. Plunges head first into water to catch fish. 92cm.

➡ CORMORANT
Seen near the sea but also at inland lakes.
Some have grey head and neck in breeding season. Nests in colonies. 92cm.

White patch in breeding season

GEESE

➡ BRENT GOOSE
Look for this small, dark goose on estuaries in winter. 58cm.

Brent goose

Canada geese were brought here from N. America

⬅ CANADA GOOSE
A large, noisy goose. Look in parks. Nests wild in Britain. 95cm.

➡ GREYLAG GOOSE
Nests wild in Scotland and others have been released further south. Wild birds from Iceland visit Scotland in winter. 82cm.

Barnacle goose has more white on head than Canada goose

⬅ BARNACLE GOOSE
Look for Barnacle geese on the west coasts of Britain and Ireland in winter. Feeds in flocks on farmland. 63cm.

12

GEESE, SWANS

➡ PINK-FOOTED GOOSE
A winter visitor. Seen in large numbers on fields in Scotland and near coasts in England. 68cm.

◀ BEAN GOOSE
A rare winter visitor from northern Europe. Grazes on farmland away from the coast. 80cm.

➡ WHITE-FRONTED GOOSE
A winter visitor to estuaries, marshes and farmland. Look for white at base of bill. 72cm.

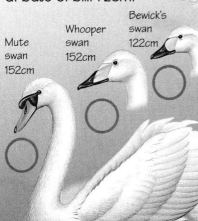

Mute swan 152cm

Whooper swan 152cm

Bewick's swan 122cm

◀ SWANS
Mute swans are often seen in parks or on rivers. The others come to Britain in winter and can be seen on lakes or flooded fields.

DUCKS

Mallard   Teal   Wigeon

◄ MALLARD
Found near most inland waters. Only the female, gives the familiar "quack". 58cm.

➡ TEAL
Smallest European duck. A very shy bird. It prefers the shallow edges of lakes. Flies with fast wing beats. 35cm.

◄ WIGEON
Sometimes seen grazing on fields near water. Forms flocks in winter especially near the sea. Male's call is a loud "wheeo". 46cm.

➡ PINTAIL
Uses its long neck to feed on plants under the water. Look for these birds in winter, often near sea. 66cm.

Pintail   Shoveler   Pochard   Tufted   Eider
                                  duck   duck

➡ SHOVELER

Likes quiet lakes and shallow water. Uses its long, flat bill to filter food from the surface of the water Call is low "quack". 51cm.

⬅ POCHARD

Spends much of its time resting on open water and dives for food. More likely to be seen in winter. 46cm.

➡ TUFTED DUCK

Another diving duck which is more common in winter. Can sometimes be seen on park lakes. 43cm.

⬅ EIDER

Breeds around rocky northern coasts. Forms large flocks on the sea in winter. 58cm.

15

DUCKS

➡ GOLDENEYE
A few nest in Scotland, but mainly a winter visitor from northern Europe. Seen on the sea and inland lakes, often in small flocks. Dives frequently. 46cm.

⬅ RED-BREASTED MERGANSER
Breeds by lakes and rivers. Seldom seen inland in winter, but visits many coastal areas and open sea. Dives for fish. 58cm.

➡ GOOSANDER
Most British goosanders nest in the north and west. Likes large lakes in winter. Dives for fish. Look for shaggy crest on female. 66cm.

Female has no lump on bill

⬅ SHELDUCK
Common around most sandy coasts, especially estuaries. Often in flocks. Groups of young join together in late summer. Looks slow and heavy in flight. 61cm.

GREBES, HERON, STORK

➡ GREAT CRESTED GREBE

Found on inland waters. Dives for fish. Beautiful courtship displays in spring. May be seen on sea in winter. 48cm.

Crest expands during display

Winter

Summer

Winter

Summer

⬅ LITTLE GREBE OR DABCHICK

Common on inland waters, but secretive and hard to spot. Call is a shrill trill. 27cm.

➡ GREY HERON

Usually seen near water. Nests in colonies in trees. Eats fish, frogs and small mammals. 92cm.

Head drawn back and legs stick out when flying

⬅ WHITE STORK

Very rare in Britain. Likes wet areas. Will nest on buldings and pylons in Europe. 102cm.

BIRDS OF PREY

➡ OSPREY
Rare summer visitor to Britain. Some nest in Scotland but seen further south on its migration to Africa. Plunges into water to catch fish. 56cm.

Upper parts are dark brown

Wings narrower than buzzard's

Long broad wings

⬅ GOLDEN EAGLE
Lives in Scottish Highlands. Young birds have white on wings and tail. Glides for long distances. Bigger than buzzard. 83cm.

➡ RED KITE
This rare bird nests in oak woods in mid Wales. Recently released in Scotland and England and increasing in numbers. Soars for long periods. 62cm.

Long forked tail

Notice the pale wing patches

← BUZZARD
Large bird of prey with broad wings. Often seen soaring over moors and farmland as it hunts. Rarer in south and eastern England. 54cm.

Female is larger and browner than male

♀

→ SPARROWHAWK
Broad-winged hawk. Hunts small birds along hedges and woodland edges. Never hovers. Male 30cm. Female 38cm.

♂

Long pointed wings and tail

♀

♂

← KESTREL
Well-known for the way it hovers when hunting, especially alongside motorways. Some nest in towns. Eats birds, insects and small mammals. 34cm.

BIRDS OF PREY

➡ HOBBY
Catches large insects and birds in the air. Summer visitor to southern England. Look on heaths and near water. 33cm.

Tail shorter and wings longer than kestrel

⬅ GOSHAWK
Looks like a large sparrowhawk. Lives in woods. Rare in Britain. Male 48cm. Female 58cm.

➡ PEREGRINE
Sea cliffs or inland crags. Hunts over estuaries and marshes in winter. Dives on flying birds at great speed. 38-48cm.

⬅ HONEY BUZZARD
Summer visitor to British woodlands. Eats mainly grubs of wasps and bees. Rare. 51-59cm.

RAILS, CRAKE

➡ MOORHEN
A water bird that lives near ponds, lakes or streams. Notice red bill and white tail. Young are brown. 33cm.

⬅ COOT
Dives a lot. Prefers large lakes. Look for white bill and forehead. Young are grey with pale throats and breasts. Flocks in winter. 38cm.

➡ CORNCRAKE
Difficult to see as it lives in long grass. Repeats "crex-crex" cry monotonously, especially after dark. Rare in Britain. 27cm.

⬅ WATER RAIL
Secretive bird that lives in reed beds. Listen for its piglet-like squeal. Legs trail in flight. Swims for short distances. 28cm.

21

GAME BIRDS

➡ RED GROUSE
➡ WILLOW GROUSE

Red grouse lives on moors in Britain. Willow grouse lives in northern Europe. Willow grouse is white in winter. 36cm.

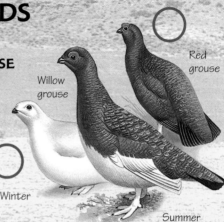

Red grouse

Willow grouse

Winter

Summer

In summer, the male's plumage is browner and the female's yellower than in autumn

Winter

⬅ PTARMIGAN
Lives on barren mountain tops in the north. Has three different plumages and is well camouflaged. Allows people to get close. 34cm.

Autumn

➡ BLACK GROUSE
Found on edge of moorland, sometimes perched in trees. Groups of males display together at an area known as a "lek". Male 53cm. Female 41cm.

♂

♀

➡ CAPERCAILLIE
Lives in pine forests in parts of Scotland. Eats pine shoots at tips of branches. Male 86cm. Female 61cm.

♂

♀

⬅ GREY PARTRIDGE
Often in small groups. Likes farmland with hedges. Its call is a grating "kirr-ic". Rare in Ireland. 30cm.

➡ PHEASANT
Lives on farmland with hedges. Often reared as game. Roosts in trees. Nests on ground. Male 87cm. Female 58cm.

Look for long tail

♂

Males can vary in colour and often have a white neck ring

♀

⬅ RED-LEGGED PARTRIDGE
Common in southern and eastern Britain. Fields and open sandy areas. Often runs rather than flies. 34cm.

WADERS

White collar in winter

◄ OYSTERCATCHER
Usually seen near the sea, especially in winter. Nests inland in Scotland and parts of England. Feeds on shellfish. 43cm.

Summer

White wing bars show in flight

➤ LAPWING
A farmland bird which flocks in winter. Looks black and white from a distance. Displays in the air in breeding season. Calls "pee-wit". 30cm.

Broad, rounded wings

Summer

◄ TURNSTONE
Likes shingle or rocky shores. Turns stones over to find food. Does not nest in Britain, but can be seen most months. 23cm.

Winter

➡ RINGED PLOVER

Usually found near the sea, but sometimes by inland lakes. Likes sandy or shingle shores. Seen all the year round. 19cm.

Summer

Juvenile

Broad white bar on wing

Adult

Notice yellow eye-ring

⬅ LITTLE RINGED PLOVER

Summer visitor. Most common in southeast England. Likes gravel pits and shingle banks inland. Legs are yellowish. 15cm.

Golden plover in winter

Northern Europe

➡ GOLDEN PLOVER

Breeds on upland moors, but found in flocks on coastal marshes or lowland farms in winter. 28cm.

Southern Europe

WADERS

➡ REDSHANK
Breeds on sea shores and
wet meadows. Look for
white on rump and
back edges of wings
in flight. 28cm.

Red legs

⬅ GREENSHANK
Rarer and slightly bigger
than redshank. Seen in
spring and autumn on
coasts or inland. Some
nest in northern
Scotland. 30cm.

**➡ COMMON
SANDPIPER**
Summer visitor to upland
streams and lakes. Visits
wet areas in lowland Britain
in spring and autumn.
Wags tail and bobs. 20cm.

Winter

Summer

White
wing bar

Summer

**⬅ BLACK-TAILED
GODWIT**
A few nest in
wet meadows in Britain,
but more seen on
coasts during
autumn and
winter. 41cm.

➡ BAR-TAILED GODWIT
Smaller than black-tailed
godwit. Most are seen in
spring and autumn, but
some winter on east coast
mud flats or estuaries. 37cm.

Winter

Pale rump

No wing bar

⬅ CURLEW
Britain's largest
wader. Nests on moors
and upland farmland.
Seen on coasts at other
times of year. Song is
"courli". 48-64cm.

Look for
stripe on
head

Bill shorter
than
curlew's

➡ WHIMBREL
Like a small curlew. A few
nest in heather in northern
Scotland. Many more visit
Britain's coasts in spring
and autumn. 40cm.

27

WADERS

Winter

Summer

← DUNLIN
A common vsitor to
sea shores, but nests
on moorland in the
north. Often seen in
flocks. Beak straight or
down-curved. 19cm.

Winter

➡ KNOT
Seen in huge flocks in
winter. Likes sand or mud
flats in estuaries. Rare
inland. Mainly a winter
visitor. Breeds in the
Arctic. 25cm.

← SANDERLING
Seen on coasts in winter.
Runs along water's
edge on sandy beaches
where it catches small
animals washed up by
waves. 20cm.

Winter

Summer

♂

♀

➡ RUFF
Seen in autumn and
spring, but also winter
in wet places and a
few stay to nest. Male
29cm. Female 23cm.

Winter

28

➡ WOODCOCK

Secretive bird of damp woods. Watch out for its bat-like display flight over woods at dusk in early summer. 34cm.

Snipe in flight

Woodcock in flight

⬅ SNIPE

Lives in wet fields, marshes or lake edges. Hard to see on the ground, but rises up with a zig-zag flight when disturbed. 27cm.

➡ AVOCET

Nests on coastal marshes in eastern England. Flocks winter on southern estuaries. Rare inland. 43cm.

PIGEONS, DOVES

➤ WOODPIGEON
Largest of the pigeons. Common on farmland and in woods and towns. Forms large flocks. 41cm.

White on wings

Grey rump. No white on wings

◄ STOCK DOVE
Nests in holes in trees or in rock faces. Feeds on the ground, often with woodpigeons. Sometimes seen in flocks. 33cm.

➤ ROCK DOVE
➤ TOWN PIGEON
Town pigeons are descended from rock doves which are usually found in small groups on sea cliffs. 33cm.

Town pigeons   White rump

White on tail

◄ COLLARED DOVE
Found in parks, large gardens, or near farm buildings. Feeds mainly on grain. 30cm.

➤ TURTLE DOVE
Summer visitor to England and Wales. Woods, parks and farmland. Listen for purring call. 28cm.

White edge to tail

AUKS, FULMAR

Neck and throat are white in winter

Summer

← RAZORBILL
Look for its flat-sided bill. Nests on cliffs and rocky shores in colonies. Winters at sea. Dives for fish. Often with guillemots. 41cm.

Neck and throat are white in winter

→ GUILLEMOT
Nests on cliffs in large groups. Slimmer than razorbill. Northern birds have white eye-ring and line on heads. 42cm.

Summer

← FULMAR
Nests in colonies on ledges on sea cliffs. Often glides close to the waves on stiff wings. Can be seen near cliffs all round our coasts. 47cm.

→ PUFFIN
Rocky islands and sea cliffs in the north and west. Nests between rocks or in burrows in the ground. 30cm.

Colourful beak and reddish feet in summer

GULLS

➡ BLACK-HEADED GULL
Common near the sea and inland. Nests in colonies. Look for white front edge of long wings. 37cm.

Winter

Dark brown head in summer only

⬅ LESSER BLACK-BACKED GULL
Mainly summer visitor to coasts or inland. Some winter in Britain. Head streaked with grey in winter. 53cm.

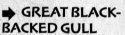

Legs yellow in summer

➡ GREAT BLACK-BACKED GULL
Britain's largest gull. Not very common inland. Nests on rocky coasts. Often solitary. Legs pinkish. 66cm.

⬅ COMMON GULL
Some nest in Scotland and Ireland. Seen further south and often inland in winter. 41cm.

GULL, TERNS

Summer

◀ HERRING GULL
Common in ports and seaside towns. Scrounges food from people and even nests on buildings. Young's plumage is mottled brown for first three years. 56cm.

Arctic tern in summer

➤ ARCTIC TERN,
➤ COMMON TERN
Both species most likely to be seen near the sea, but common tern also nests inland. Both dive into water to catch fish. 34cm.

Summer

Common tern's bill has black tip

◀ BLACK TERN
A spring and autumn visitor. Can be seen flying low over lakes, dipping down to pick food from surface. 24cm.

Summer

Autumn

➤ LITTLE TERN
Summer visitor. Nests in small groups on shingle beaches. Dives for fish. 24cm.

Yellow bill with black tip

Summer

OWLS

➡ BARN OWL
Its call is an eerie shriek.
Often nests in old
buildings or hollow trees.
Hunts small mammals
and roosting birds
at night. 34cm.

Birds with dark
faces and breasts
are found in north
and east Europe

Bouncing
flight

⬅ LITTLE OWL
Small, flat-headed owl.
Flies low over farmland
and hunts at dusk. Nests
in tree-holes. Bobs up and
down when curious. 22cm.

➡ TAWNY OWL
Calls with familiar "hoot".
Hunts at night where
there are woods or
old trees. Eats small
mammals or birds.
38cm.

⬅ PYGMY OWL
The smallest European
owl. Found in mountain
forests, but not in Britain.
Has a whistling "keeoo"
call. Hunts small birds in
flight. 16cm.

➡ SHORT-EARED OWL

Hunts small mammals in daylight and at dusk. Likes open country. Perches on the ground. Fierce-looking. 37cm.

⬅ LONG-EARED OWL

A secretive night-hunting owl of thick pine woods. Roosts during the day. Long "ear" tufts cannot be seen in flight. 34cm.

➡ TENGMALM'S OWL

Small owl that lives in northern and central European forests. Very rare visitor to Britain. Hunts at night. Nests in tree-holes. 25cm.

⬅ SCOPS OWL

Very rare visitor from southern Europe. Gives monotonous "kiu" call from hidden perch. Hunts only at night. 19cm.

HOOPOE, NIGHTJAR, CUCKOO, KINGFISHER

➡ HOOPOE
Rare visitor to Britain, seen mainly in spring. More common in southern Europe. Probes ground for insects with its long bill. 28cm.

⬅ NIGHTJAR
Rarely seen in daylight. Listen for churring call at night when it hunts insects. Summer migrant to heathland. 27cm.

Male has white spots on wings

➡ CUCKOO
Male's song well known. Female has bubbling call. Found all over Britain in summer. Looks like a sparrowhawk in flight. 30cm.

Juvenile Cuckoo

⬅ KINGFISHER
Small and brilliantly coloured. Seen near lakes and rivers. Dives for fish. Listen for shrill whistle. 17cm.

Usually flies low and straight over water

WOODPECKERS

➡ BLACK WOODPECKER

Size of a rook. Found in forests in Europe, especially old pine woods, but not in Britain. Can be confused with crow in flight. 46cm.

Male (shown here) has red crown. Female has red patch on back of head.

Large white patches on wings

⬅ GREAT SPOTTED WOODPECKER

Size of a blackbird. Found in woods all over Britain. Drums on trees in spring. 23cm.

➡ LESSER SPOTTED WOODPECKER

Sparrow-sized. Lacks white wing patches of great spotted woodpecker. Male has red crown. Open woodland. Not in Scotland. 14cm.

Striped back

Yellow-green rump

⬅ GREEN WOODPECKER

Pigeon-sized. Often feeds on ground. Open woods and parks. Quite common in England and Wales. Rare in Scotland. Has a laugh-like call. 32cm.

Woodpeckers do not live in Ireland. They all have bouncing flight

SWIFT, SWALLOW, MARTINS

➡ SWIFT

A common migrant that visits Britain from May to August. Flies fast over towns and country, often in flocks. Listen for its screaming call. 17cm.

Swift's tail is forked

Catches insects in flight

Swallow's tail has streamers when adult

⬅ SWALLOW

Summer migrant, seen from April to October. Prefers country, often near water. Nests on rafters or ledges in buldings. 19cm.

White rump

White underparts

➡ HOUSE MARTIN

Summer migrant. Builds cup-shaped nest under eaves. Found in town and country. Catches insects in flight. 13cm.

Brown back

Brown band on breast

⬅ SAND MARTIN

Summer migrant. Groups nest in holes in sandy cliffs and other soft banks. Often seen in flocks, catching insects over water. 12cm.

LARKS, PIPITS, DUNNOCK

White outer tail feathers

Pale back edges to wings

← SKYLARK
Lives in open country, especially farmland. Rises to a great height, hovers, and sails down, singing. 18cm.

Orange outer tail feathers

➡ CRESTED LARK
Not often in Britain, but widespread in central and southern Europe. Open, often barren, areas. 17cm.

← MEADOW PIPIT
Most common on upland moors, but also in fields, marshes and other open areas, especially in winter. 14.5cm.

➡ TREE PIPIT
Summer migrant to heaths and places with scattered trees or bushes. Often perches on branches. 15cm.

← DUNNOCK
Common, even in gardens. Feeds under bird tables. Mouse-like walk. Often flicks wings. 14.5cm.

WAGTAILS

➤ PIED WAGTAIL
➤ WHITE WAGTAIL

The white wagtail is widespread in Europe, but only the pied wagtail is usually seen in Britain. Common, even in towns. 18cm.

Pied wagtail

Juveniles of both kinds are grey

White wagtail

◀ GREY WAGTAIL

Usually nests near fast-flowing water in hilly areas. Paler yellow in winter, when it visits lowland waters. 18cm.

Male has black throat

♂ Summer

Blue-headed wagtail, central Europe ♂

Yellow wagtail, Britain and Ireland ♂

➤ BLUE-HEADED WAGTAIL
➤ YELLOW WAGTAIL

Two different forms of the same species. Summer visitor to grassy places near water. Yellow wagtail only seen in Britain. 17cm.

Spanish wagtail, Spain and Portugal ♂

Ashy-headed wagtail, southern Europe ♂

40   All the birds on this page wag their tails up and down

WAXWING, DIPPER, WREN, SHRIKES

Resembles a
starling in flight

← WAXWING
Rare winter visitor from
northern Europe. Feeds on
berries. May be seen in
towns. 17cm.

→ DIPPER
Fast-flowing rivers and
streams in hilly areas.
Bobs up and down
on rocks in water.
Walks underwater to
find food.
18cm.

Northern
Europe

Britain and
central
Europe

Flies fast and
straight on tiny,
rounded wings

← WREN
Very small. Found almost
everywhere. Loud song
finishes with a trill. Never
still for long. 9.5cm.

♂ ♀

**→ RED-
BACKED SHRIKE**
Rare visitor to Britain.
Catches and eats
insects, small birds,
etc. 17cm.

Sticks
food on
thorns to
store it

**← GREAT
GREY SHRIKE**
Winter visitor to open
country in Britain. Feeds
on birds and mammals.
Often hovers. 24cm.

WARBLERS

➡ SEDGE WARBLER
Summer migrant. Nests in thick vegetation, usually near water, but also in drier areas. Sings from cover and is often difficult to see. 13cm.

White stripe over eye

Reddish-brown rump

⬅ REED WARBLER
Summer visitor. Nests in reed beds or among waterside plants, mainly in the south of England. Hard to spot. Look for it flitting over reeds. 13cm.

➡ GARDEN WARBLER
Summer visitor. Sings from dense cover and is hard to see. Likes undergrowth or thick hedges. Song can be confused with blackcap's. 14cm.

Brown above, paler below

♂

Female's cap is reddish-brown

♀

⬅ BLACKCAP
Common summer visitor to woods or places with trees. Always moving from perch to perch as it sings. 14cm.

Male has grey head and white
throat. Females and young
have brown heads

♂

➡ WILLOW WARBLER
Summer migrant.
Commonest British
warbler. Its song, which
comes down the scale, is
the best way of telling it
from the chiffchaff. 11cm.

Dark
legs

➡ WOOD WARBLER
Summer migrant to open
woods. Sings from a
branch, repeating a note
faster and faster until it
becomes a trill. 13cm.

⬅ WHITETHROAT
A summer migrant, which
hides itself in thick, low
bushes. Sometimes sings
its fast, scratchy song in
flight. Flight is short and
jerky. 14cm.

Pale legs

⬅ CHIFFCHAFF
Summer migrant,
often arriving in March.
A few spend the winter
in Britain. Its repetitive
"chiff-chaff" song can
be heard in woods and
from bushes. 11cm.

Yellow
breast,
white
underparts

43

FLYCATCHERS, CHATS

◀ PIED FLYCATCHER
Catches insects in air. Also
feeds on the ground.
Summer migrant to old
woodland. 13cm.

➡ WHINCHAT
Summer migrant, found in
open country. "Tic-tic"
call. Perches on tops of
bushes and posts. 13cm.

Flicks
wings
and tail

◀ STONECHAT
"Tac-tac" call sounds like
stones being knocked
together. Found on heaths
with gorse, especially
near the sea. 13cm.

Colour is
duller in
winter

➡ WHEATEAR
Summer migrant to
moors and barren
areas, but also seen
elsewhere in the spring
and autumn. 15cm.

White rump
and black tail

➡ SPOTTED FLYCATCHER

Summer migrant. Likes open woods, parks and country gardens. Catches insects in flight. 14cm.

Sits upright, often on a bare branch

♀

⬅ REDSTART

A summer migrant to open woods, heaths and parks. Constantly flickers its tail. 14cm.

♀

♂

➡ BLACK REDSTART

A few nest on buldings or on cliffs in Britain. Some winter in south of England. Flickers its tail. 14cm.

Male and female look alike

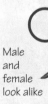

⬅ ROBIN

Woodland bird that is familiar in gardens. Sings in winter and spring. "Tic-tic"is its call of alarm. 14cm.

Reddish tail

➡ NIGHTINGALE

Secretive summer migrant. Best found by listening for its song in May and June. 17cm.

THRUSHES, ORIOLE

➡ FIELDFARE
Winter visitor, but a few nest in England and Scotland. Flocks can be seen in autumn, eating berries. 25.5cm.

◀ RING OUZEL
Summer migrant to moors and mountains. Visits lower areas on migration. Shyer than blackbird. Loud piping call. 24cm.

♀

♂

Young are lighter and spottier than female
♀

➡ BLACKBIRD
Lives where there are trees and bushes, often in parks and gardens. Loud musical song. Clucking alarm call. 25cm.

♂

◀ GOLDEN ORIOLE
Rare summer migrant most often seen in woods of eastern England. Hard to see as it spends a lot of time in tree-tops. 24cm.

♂

♀

THRUSHES, STARLING

◀ REDWING
Winter migrant, but a few nest in Scotland. Feeds on berries in hedges and hunts worms. 21cm.

White stripe over eye

➡ SONG THRUSH
Found near or in trees or bushes. Well-known for the way it breaks open snail shells. Often in gardens. 23cm.

Smaller than mistle thrush

◀ MISTLE THRUSH
Large thrush found in most parts of Britain. Seen on the ground in fields and on moors. 27cm.

White under wing

White outer tail feathers

➡ STARLING
A familiar garden bird. Often roosts in huge flocks. Mimics songs of other birds. 22cm.

Adult in winter

Juvenile

TITS

➡ LONG-TAILED TIT
Hedgerows and the edges of woods are good places to see groups of these tiny birds. 14cm.

Northern and eastern Europe

Britain and western Europe

⬅ CRESTED TIT
Widespread in Europe but in Britain only found in a few Scottish pine woods, especially in the Spey Valley. 11cm.

➡ COAL TIT
Likes conifer woods, but often seen in deciduous trees. Large white patch on back of head. 11cm.

⬅ BLUE TIT
Seen in woods and gardens. Often raises its blue cap to form a small crest. Young are less colourful. 11cm.

No pale patch on wings

➡ MARSH TIT
A bird of decidous woods, like the willow tit (not illustrated). Rarely visits gardens. 11cm.

TIT, NUTHATCH, CRESTS, TREECREEPER

➡ GREAT TIT
Largest tit. Lives in woodlands and gardens. Nests in holes in trees or will use nestboxes. 14cm.

Broad black band on breast

⬅ NUTHATCH
Deciduous woods in England and Wales. Climbs up and down trees in a series of short hops. Very short tail. Nests in tree-holes. 14cm.

➡ TREECREEPER
Usually seen in woods climbing up tree trunks and flying down again to search for food. Listen for high-pitched call. 13cm.

Firecrest

White stripe over eye

Goldcrest

⬅ FIRECREST
⬅ GOLDCREST
Smallest European birds. Goldcrests are found in woods, especially of pine, all over Britain. Firecrests are much rarer. 9cm.

FINCHES

➡ CHAFFINCH
Found in gardens and wherever there are trees and bushes. Often seen in flocks on farmland in winter. 15cm.

♀

Male's head is brown in winter

♀

♂

◀ BRAMBLING
Winter migrant from northern Europe. Flocks feed on grain and seeds. Likes fruit from beech trees. 15cm.

➡ GREENFINCH
A frequent visitor to gardens, especially in winter. Likely to nest wherever there are trees and bushes. 15cm.

♀

♂

♀

♂

◀ SISKIN
A small finch which nests in conifers. It sometimes visits gardens in winter to feed on peanuts. 11cm.

← BULLFINCH

Secretive bird often found on edges of woods, and in hedges or gardens. Eats seeds and also buds from fruit trees. 15cm.

White rump
shows in flight

→ LINNET

Lives on heathland and farmland, but also found in towns, where it may visit gardens. Feeds on the seeds of weeds. Flocks in winter. 13cm.

Lesser
Redpoll

← LESSER REDPOLL
← MEALY REDPOLL

The lesser redpoll is common in birch woods and forestry plantations in Britain. The mealy redpoll lives in northern Europe. 12cm.

Mealy
Redpoll

→ GOLDFINCH

Feeds on thistle seeds and other weed seeds in open places. Nests in trees. 12cm.

Yellow
wing
bar

CROSSBILL, CROWS

♀ ♂

← CROSSBILL
Nests in pine woods. A slightly different species nests in Scotland. Eats pine cone seeds. 16cm.

Crossbills are sparrow-sized, with large heads and bills

➡ JAY
Secretive woodland bird. Will visit gardens. Listen for harsh screeching call. Look for white rump in flight. 32cm.

← RAVEN
This large crow lives in wild rocky areas or on rocky coasts. Look for its wedge-shaped tail and huge bill. Croaks. 64cm.

➡ JACKDAW
Small member of the crow family. Found where there are old trees, old buildings, or cliffs. Nests in colonies. Often seen with rooks. 33cm.

← CARRION CROW
← HOODED CROW
Carrion is more often seen alone or in pairs. Hooded crows form flocks. Carrion is more widespread than hooded. 47cm.

Carrion crow - England, Wales and Southern Scotland

Hooded crow - northern Scotland and Ireland

➡ ROOK
Nests in "rookeries" in tops of trees. Is usually seen in flocks on farmland. Young lack bare skin round beak. Call is harsh "kaw". 46cm.

Baggy thigh feathers

← MAGPIE
Seen in both town and country. Eats many eggs and young birds in spring. Long tail is very noticeable in flight. 46cm.

SPARROWS, BUNTINGS

➡ HOUSE SPARROW
Very familiar bird. Lives near houses and even in city centres, where it eats scraps, etc. Often seen in flocks. 15cm.

♂ ♀

Brown cap and smudge below eye

Male and female look alike

➡ YELLOWHAMMER
Found in open country, especially farmland. Feeds on ground. Forms flocks in winter. Sings from the tops of bushes. 17cm.

⬅ TREE SPARROW
Usually nests in holes in trees or cliffs. Much less common than house sparrow. 14cm.

♂ ♀

♀

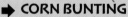

♀

♂

⬅ REED BUNTING
Most common near water, but some nest in dry areas with long grass. May visit bird tables in winter. 15cm.

➡ CORN BUNTING
Nests in cornfields. Sings from posts, bushes or overhead wires. 18cm.

FEEDING BIRDS

You can encourage birds to visit a windowsill or garden by putting out food. The best time to feed birds is in the winter when natural food is in short supply. In the spring only put out wild bird seed (from a pet shop) as baby birds need mainly foods such as grubs and insects.

Blue tit feeding on peanuts

WHAT TO FEED BIRDS

Cheese, fat, nuts, dried fruit and baked potatoes (cut in half) are all good for providing a high-energy diet for birds. Raw, unsalted peanuts are popular. You can also buy wild bird seed from pet shops. Remember to clear and clean bird tables and bird-feeders at regular intervals.

WATER

If you put out food, you should also provide water for drinking and bathing. A large dish, or an old dustbin lid on bricks makes a simple bird bath. Don't forget to break the ice in cold weather and clean the bath regularly.

MAKE A BIRD CAKE

You can make a bird cake from seeds, nuts, oatmeal and dried fruit. Put 500g of the mixture in a heat-resistant bowl. Melt 250g of solid fat in a saucepan over a low heat. Carefully pour the fat over the mixture and leave to set.

Turn the cake out when it is cold. Put it on a bird table or feeding station whole.

MAKE A BIRD-FEEDER

To make a simple bird-feeder you need two clean, empty cartons, a pencil, some scissors, a stapler and some garden wire.

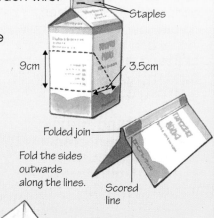

1. Use the stapler to close up the top of one carton. Draw and cut along the dotted lines shown here.

Staples

9cm

3.5cm

2. Cut two sides from the other carton, leaving them joined. Use scissors to score a line 1cm each side of the join. Fold along these lines to make the roof.

Folded join

Fold the sides outwards along the lines.

Scored line

Drainage holes

Wire

Staple

Roof

3. Make two drainage holes in the base. Then staple on the roof, making sure it overhangs the holes. Push the pencil through the feeder to make a perch.

Overhang

4. Use the wire to hang the feeder from a bird table or tree. If you don't have a garden, hang the feeder from a bracket fixed to an outside window frame, but get permission to attach the bracket first.

Pencil

USEFUL WORDS

This list explains some of the terms used in this book. Words in *italics* are defined separately.

bar – a natural mark across a feather or group of feathers.

belly – part of a bird's body between its *breast* and tail.

bill – another word for beak.

bird of prey – a bird such as an eagle which hunts other animals for food.

breast – part of a bird's body between its throat and *belly.*

breeding season – the time of year when a pair of birds build a nest, mate, lay eggs and look after their young. In Britain this is usually spring.

colony – a group of birds of the same species nesting close together.

conifers – trees such as pines and firs that have cones, and needle-shaped leaves.

courtship display – when a male bird attracts a mate. Some birds show off their *plumage*; others do a "display" in the air.

cover – anywhere that birds hide themselves - hedges, bushes, thick grass, etc.

crown – the top part of a bird's head.

flock – a group of birds of the same *species* feeding or travelling together

game bird – a bird such as a pheasant or partridge that is hunted by humans for food.

habitat – the place where a *species* of bird lives.

hover – when a bird stays in one place in the air by flapping its wings very fast.

juvenile – a young bird that does not yet have full, adult *plumage.*

lek – an area where the male birds of some *species* gather to perform a *courtship display* to females.

migration – a regular movement of birds from one place to another, from the breeding area to the area where they spend the winter. Migrating birds are called migrants or visitors.

moult – when birds lose their old feathers and grow new ones. All birds do this at least once a year.

nape – the back of a bird's neck.

perch – when a bird stands on a branch, etc. by gripping with its toes; or the place where a bird perches.

plumage – a bird's feathers.

primaries – the large, outer wing feathers.

roost – when a bird sleeps; or a place where birds sleep.

rump – the area of a bird's body above its tail.

secondaries – the inner wing feathers.

species – a group of birds that all look alike and behave in the same way, e.g. herring gull is the name of one species.

wader – one of a group of long-legged birds that live near water and often wade in search of food.

GOING FURTHER

If you have access to the Internet, you can visit these Web sites to find out more about birds and birdwatching. For links to these sites, go to the Usborne Quicklinks Web site at **www.usborne-quicklinks.com** and enter the keywords "spotters birds".

Internet safety

When using the Internet, please follow the **Internet safety guidelines** shown on the Usborne Quicklinks Web site.

WEB SITE 1 The Web site of the RSPB, the Royal Society for the Protection of Birds (see opposite page for more information).

WEB SITE 2 A young, friendly Web site with information on different bird species, bird anatomy, bird facts, and lots of things to make and do.

WEB SITE 3 Information about rare sightings and articles by well-known birdwatchers.

WEB SITE 4 Species profiles, a photo gallery and a reference section with information on bird care.

WEB SITE 5 Detailed information about how birds fly.

WEB SITE 6 Owls of the world with sound clips of their calls.

WEB SITE 7 Everything you need to know about the wildlife of wetlands.

WEB SITE 8 Listen to bird songs and find out how to make recordings.

WEB SITE 9 Information for UK birdwatchers with news of rare sightings and tips for identifying birds.

WEB SITE 10 The Worldwide Fund for Nature. (You can search this site for information about birds.)

WEB SITE 11 Tips and ideas to help you have fun watching birds.

WEB SITE 12 Links to Web sites all over the world where you can see nesting birds via Web cams.

WEB SITE 13 - RSPB Youth section.

JOIN THE RSPB WILDLIFE EXPLORERS

If you want to find out more about birds and other wildlife, become a member of the RSPB Wildlife Explorers, the junior section of the RSPB (the Royal Society for the Protection of Birds). Joining the RSPB Wildlife Explorers will give you the chance to take part in projects and competitions and meet other people who share your interest. This is what you will get when you join:

- Your own membership card.
- Free entry to more than 120 RSPB nature reserves.
- *Bird Life* magazine packed with photos, articles and things to do and make, six times a year.
- The chance to join activity days, holidays and local groups.

Find out more by writing to: RSPB Wildlife Explorers, The Lodge, Sandy, Bedfordshire SG19 2DL, or telephone: 01767 680551, or go to Usborne Quicklinks at **www.usborne-quicklinks.com** and click on **Web site 13** for a link to the RSPB Youth Web site.

SCORECARD

The birds on this scorecard are in alphabetical order. Fill in the date on which you spot a bird beside its name. A common bird scores 5 points, and a rare one is worth 25. After a day's spotting, add up the points you have scored on a sheet of paper and keep a record of them. See if you can score more points another day.

Species (Name of bird)	Score	Date spotted	Species (Name of bird)	Score	Date spotted
Arctic tern	15		Brambling	15	
Avocet	20		Brent goose	20	
Barnacle goose	20		Bullfinch	15	
Barn owl	15		Buzzard	15	
Bar-tailed godwit	20		Canada goose	5	
Bean goose	25		Capercaillie	25	
Bewick's swan	20		Carrion crow	5	
Blackbird	5		Chaffinch	5	
Blackcap	15		Chiffchaff	10	
Black grouse	20		Coal tit	10	
Black-headed gull	5		Collared dove	5	
Black redstart	20		Common gull	15	
Black-tailed godwit	20		Common sandpiper	15	
Black tern	20		Common tern	15	
Black woodpecker	25		Coot	10	
Blue-headed wagtail	25		Cormorant	10	
Blue tit	5		Corn bunting	15	

Species (Name of bird)	Score	Date spotted	Species (Name of bird)	Score	Date spotted
Corncrake	25		Great grey shrike	25	
Crested lark	25		Great spotted woodpecker	10	
Crested tit	20		Great tit	5	
Crossbill	20		Greenfinch	10	
Cuckoo	10		Greenshank	20	
Curlew	15		Green woodpecker	15	
Dipper	15		Grey heron	10	
Dunlin	10		Greylag goose	10	
Dunnock	5		Grey partridge	15	
Eider	15		Grey wagtail	15	
Fieldfare	10		Guillemot	15	
Firecrest	25		Herring gull	5	
Fulmar	10		Hobby	20	
Gannet	15		Honey buzzard	25	
Garden warbler	15		Hooded crow	10	
Goldcrest	10		Hoopoe	25	
Golden eagle	25		House martin	10	
Goldeneye	15		House sparrow	5	
Golden oriole	25		Jackdaw	10	
Golden plover	15		Jay	10	
Goldfinch	10		Kestrel	10	
Goosander	20		Kingfisher	15	
Goshawk	25		Knot	15	
Great black-backed gull	15		Lapwing	10	
Great crested grebe	10		Lesser black-backed gull	10	

Species (Name of bird)	Score	Date spotted	Species (Name of bird)	Score	Date spotted
Lesser redpoll	15		Pied wagtail	10	
Lesser spotted woodpecker	20		Pink-footed goose	20	
Linnet	10		Pintail	20	
Little grebe	15		Pochard	15	
Little owl	15		Ptarmigan	20	
Little ringed plover	20		Puffin	20	
Little tern	20		Pygmy owl	25	
Long-eared owl	20		Raven	15	
Long-tailed tit	10		Razorbill	15	
Magpie	5		Red-backed shrike	25	
Mallard	5		Red-breasted merganser	20	
Marsh tit	15		Red grouse	15	
Meadow pipit	10		Red kite	20	
Mealy redpoll	25		Red-legged partridge	10	
Mistle thrush	10		Redshank	10	
Moorhen	5		Redstart	15	
Mute swan	10		Redwing	10	
Nightingale	15		Reed bunting	15	
Nightjar	15		Reed warbler	15	
Nuthatch	15		Ringed plover	15	
Osprey	20		Ring ouzel	15	
Oystercatcher	15		Robin	5	
Peregrine	20		Rock dove	25	
Pheasant	5		Rook	10	
Pied flycatcher	20		Ruff	20	

Species (Name of bird)	Score	Date spotted	Species (Name of bird)	Score	Date spotted
Sanderling	15		Tree sparrow	20	
Sand martin	15		Tufted duck	10	
Scops owl	25		Turnstone	15	
Sedge warbler	15		Turtle dove	15	
Shag	15		Water rail	15	
Shelduck	15		Waxwing	20	
Short-eared owl	20		Wheatear	15	
Shoveler	15		Whimbrel	20	
Siskin	15		Whinchat	15	
Skylark	10		White-fronted goose	20	
Snipe	15		White stork	25	
Song thrush	10		Whitethroat	15	
Sparrowhawk	10		White wagtail	25	
Spotted flycatcher	10		Wigeon	15	
Starling	5		Willow grouse	25	
Stock dove	15		Willow warbler	10	
Stonechat	15		Whooper swan	20	
Swallow	10		Woodcock	20	
Swift	10		Woodpigeon	5	
Tawny owl	15		Wood warbler	20	
Teal	15		Wren	5	
Tengmalm's owl	25		Yellowhammer	10	
Town pigeon	5		Yellow wagtail	15	
Treecreeper	15				
Tree pipit	15				

INDEX